THE UK AIR FRYER COOK

Many easy and delicious traditional English recipes that anyone can cook at home. Incl. tips and tricks for Beginners

Andrew J. Daniels

Introduction

Air frying is the latest culinary craze to hit both home and restaurant kitchens. Compared to traditional deep-frying, air fryers provide a healthier way of cooking your favourite fried treats. Not only do they use far less oil or fat, but they are also quicker and easier to use.

The device uses rapid air circulation to heat any food placed into it, resulting in evenly cooked dishes without the added calories and fat of oil. It effectively fries, bakes, grills, and roasts your favourite eats with a fraction of the fat and calories found in deep-fried dishes. The product is easy to use, and we can be sure that the cooking process is safe and surprisingly fast. Its design and construction make it perfect for anyone who wants to enjoy healthy, tasty snacks without sacrificing flavour. Air frying is a fantastic way to save time and energy while still eating nutritious and tasty food. From kids to adults, air fryers are sure to please everyone in the family.

In this cookbook, we will explore the exciting world of air frying. We will cover all the basics of using an air fryer to more advanced techniques. Along the way, we will provide you 100 flavourful air fryer recipes which is perfect for every day cooking. So, if you want to make delicious meals that are family-friendly and healthier than traditional deep-frying, then **THE UK AIR FRYER COOKBOOK** is a must-have kitchen staple.

How Does Air Fryer Works?

If you've been gifted your air fryer and you're not sure what it does, basically this is an appliance that cooked your food. That's the easiest way to say it. However, it's not the same as a hob or a frying pan. Regularly, you would use oil to cook your food, but with an air fryer, you literally use what it says in the name - air. That means your food is healthier and crunchier, fresher, and more delicious.

Ironically, an air fryer doesn't work by frying – the same way a deep fryer does – but more like a hot air convection oven fryer. The food in the air fryer is suspended and held in position by a perforated cooking basket. It has a powerful fan that blows hot air up through the food. This force produces a convection effect that cooks the food, making it brown and crisp.

The air fryer maintains the internal temperature at 160°C which is enough to cook breaded foods, such as frozen marinated chicken tenders or un-breaded foods, such as French fries. The air fryer cooks faster and can distribute heat more evenly compared to how many other cooking appliances work. You'll also discover that preheating does not apply to all air fryers; some don't require it, which makes them cook food faster. Unlike conventional ovens, air fryers are convenient in all seasons because they don't heat the house in warmer climates.

Choosing The Best Air Fryer Deal

There are many types air fryers on the market so you need to shop around to find the best deal. Look out for:

Cost - There are countless different devices and some will be high end, some budget options

Size - Some air fryers are quite compact whilst others are larger, check how much space you have before purchasing

Guarantee - Of course, an air fryer is an electrical device so there may be problems in the future. There are cheap air fryers without warranties, so it's best to look for a model that comes with a guarantee for peace of mind.

Brand name - Opting for a brand name doesn't necessarily mean you're getting a better device, but it does give you peace of mind, which goes a long way.

Features - Do you want a very basic device that just cooks or do you want something that will allow you to create more meals? Do your homework on features and ask questions if you need to.

You can choose an all-singing, all-dancing option or you can go for something basic. It's your choice but whichever option you go for, be sure to choose one which will allow you to create all the meals you want.

The Benefits of The Air Fryer

Buying a new kitchen gadget requires a little thought. However, an air fryer won't become a redundant device in the back of your kitchen cupboard, provided you know how to get the most out of it. Here are some of the best benefits that come with owning your very own air fryer.

- Easy and impressive food, even for beginners
- Food is cooked quickly, so perfect for those who are often on the go
- Healthier food that isn't dripping in fat
- Crispy food that has that fresh taste
- Easy to clean - many air fryers (although not all) have parts that can be dishwasher cleaned
- Your kitchen will not smell of oil!
- Cost-effective and helps you to create a huge range of different meals and snacks.

Tips to Perfect Using of An Air Fryer

Air Fryers are set to take the culinary world by storm. Offering a delicious and healthy alternative to deep fried foods, air fryers can be a great addition to any kitchen; however, they can also be a bit of a minefield to use. Luckily, there are a few essential tips and tricks to perfect using of an air fryer that can make the experience much more satisfying:

1. It is best to have the right appliances for the job. A good quality air fryer is essential for crispier and healthier results. It is also important to invest in a model with a temperature range, enabling the user to get precise cooking temperatures, ensuring food is cooked to perfection.

2. Utilize the manual. The manual that comes with your air fryer is there for a reason- so be sure to read it! In it, you will find a wealth of information on how to perfect using of an air fryer, troubleshooting tips, and even some suggested recipes to get you started. Familiarizing yourself with the manual will help you get the most out of your air fryer and will help ensure that you are using it correctly.

3. Start small. When you first start using an air fryer, it's best to experiment with a few small items first. This way, you will understand the capabilities of the fryer and make sure you are using it correctly.

4. Preheating the air fryer before adding food to it is important for maximizing the amount of heat that the food will receive. A preheated air fryer will also prevent the food from sticking to the basket, or from ending up soggy instead of crispy. Moreover, preheating the air fryer helps reduce the cooking time, further decreasing the amount of time spent on tricky kitchen tasks.

5. Experiment with the recipes. Once you have a feel for the basics, it is time to experiment with recipes. Look for ideas and recipes that call for air frying, getting creative with flavours and ingredients. This will also give you a better feel for the different settings and capabilities that your air fryer has to offer.

6. Don't overcrowd the air fryer. Too much food in the air fryer at once can cause uneven cooking and will not produce the desired results. Additionally, be sure to shake the basket halfway through cooking, if needed, to ensure even browning.

7. Keep an eye on the clock. The key to perfect air fried food is timing, so it is important to keep an eye on the clock. Depending on the size and thickness of the food, as well as the desired level of crispy-ness, cook times can vary.

8. Clean the air fryer regularly. A well-maintained air fryer will produce better results and will last longer. Be sure to clean the air fryer basket and drawer after each use, using hot, soapy water. In addition, it is important to descale the air fryer regularly, following the manufacturer's instructions.

We hope these tips and tricks will help ensure that your air fryer produces delicious and perfectly cooked food. With regular maintenance and a few simple considerations, an air fryer can help make meal preparation easier, healthier, and tastier. With these guidelines in place, you'll be well on your way to mastering the perfect use of an air fryer.

Cleaning And Maintenance

The best thing about an air fryer is that it uses a fraction of the grease a traditional fryer does. This means you'll still enjoy the crispy goodness, but healthier.
However, since you're cooking food with some amount of grease, you have some cleaning to do. You may be comfortable with the standard cleaning using soap and water but this can only do so much in terms of cleaning the baked-on grease. The homemade mixture of vinegar and baking soda can provide some assistance as it helps remove gunk. However, this will take up to 30 minutes to take effect.
It is advisable NOT to use metal utensils, abrasive sponge or steel wool to remove baked-on gunk from the air fryer. These items can cause a lot more harm than good to the non-stick coating in your air fryer.
An all-purpose cleaner might help solve the problem of cleaning your air fryer after frequent use. These non-abrasive formulas are designed to remove grease from the air fryer cooking basket and trays. They also eliminate grime and stains from the outside and inside of your appliance.

Directions for Cleaning an Air Fryer

For detailed cleaning, you can follow the manufacturer's instructions. However, the basic steps for cleaning an air fryer are quite simple and straightforward. You only need to:

1. Unplug the appliance and allow it to cool completely. To make it cool faster, remove the cooking basket and pan from the main unit.
2. Wipe the outside surface by mixing the all-purpose cleaner in a regular-sized cup of water (or as directed) in a spray bottle. Spray it on a clean damp cloth and wipe the outside surface with the cloth.
3. Clean the inside surface of the main unit by spraying the undiluted all-purpose cleaner on a clean damp cloth and use the cloth to wipe the interior. Wipe again using a plain damp clean piece of cloth.
4. Clean the coil by wiping down the heating element with the pure all-purpose cleaner to remove any stains, oil or residue. Use a plain damp cloth for the second time.
5. Wash the pans, tray and cooking basket in a dishwasher or by hand. Ensure the components are dishwasher safe before washing them. To remove baked-on grease from the removable parts, mix the all-purpose cleaner with hot water in

the sink then soak the parts for 10 minutes. Remove the soaked debris/residue/grease using a scrub brush then rinse to clean.

6. After washing, make sure the parts are completely dry before putting them back in the main unit to prevent corrosion.

BREAKFAST RECIPES

Two-Cheese Omelette

Preparation time: 5 minutes
Cooking time: 15 minutes
Servings: 4

Ingredients:
- 4 eggs
- 25ml milk
- 5ml oil
- 55g each of cubed feta & grated Cheddar cheese
- Salt & pepper to taste

Directions:
1. Preheat your air fryer to 180°C. Spray a baking tin with the oil and line the bottom with parchment.
2. Mix the eggs, milk, and all cheeses to a bowl. Pour it into your baking tin, arrange them in your basket, and air fry for 15 minutes. Fold the omelette in half

and lift it out of your fryer. Cut into 2 pieces and serve.

Nutrition: Calories 178; Fat 15g; Carbs 1g; Protein 7g

Potato & Chorizo Frittata

Preparation time: 10 minutes
Cooking time: 15 minutes
Servings: 2

Ingredients:
- 3 eggs
- 1 chorizo sausage, sliced
- 1 cubed potato, half boiled
- 40g sweetcorn, frozen
- A little olive oil
- Half a small pack of feta cheese crumbled
- A pinch of salt

Directions:
1. Add the corn, potato, and sliced chorizo, in your greased cooking basket and air fry at 180°C for 10 minutes until the sausage is browned.
2. Beat the eggs with salt in a small bowl, pour it into the grease cooking basket with the feta on top. Cook within 5 minutes, remove and serve in slices.

Nutrition: Calories 421; Fat 26g; Carbs 17g; Protein 27g

Cheese & Bacon Toasties

Preparation time: 10 minutes
Cooking time: 7 minutes
Servings: 2

Ingredients:
- 4 slices of sandwich bread
- 2 slices of cheddar cheese
- 5 slices of pre-cooked bacon
- 1 tbsp melted butter
- 2 slices of mozzarella cheese

Directions:
1. Spread the butter onto each bread slice. Place one bread slice into the air fryer basket, buttered side facing downwards. Add the cheddar, bacon, mozzarella, and slice of bread.
2. Arrange them in your cooking basket, and cook them for 4 minutes at 170ºC. Flip and cook again within 3 minutes. Serve!

Nutrition: Calories 486; Fat 26g; Carbs 25g; Protein 25g

Sprout and Bacon Hash

Preparation time: 10 minutes
Cooking time: 25 minutes
Servings: 4
Ingredients:
- 6 bacon slices, cooked & chopped
- 1 onion, chopped
- 160g Brussels sprouts, quartered
- 2 large green peppers
- 2 garlic cloves, grated
- 4 eggs
- Salt & pepper to taste
- 5ml oil

Directions:
1. Warm up your air fryer to 180°C. Spray your cooking basket with the oil.
2. Mix the bacon, onion, sprouts, green peppers, garlic, eggs, salt, and pepper in your bowl, transfer into your cooking basket and cook for 25 minutes. Cut the hash into portions and serve.

Nutrition: Calories 210; Fat 3g; Carbs 1g; Protein 4g

Egg & Ham Cups

Preparation time: 10 minutes
Cooking time: 15 minutes
Servings: 4

Ingredients:
- 4 eggs
- 8 slices of bread, pre-toasted
- 2 slices of ham
- A pinch of salt
- A pinch of pepper
- A little extra butter for greasing

Directions:
1. Grease 4 ramekins inside with butter.
2. Flatten the slices of bread using your rolling pin. Arrange the toast inside the ramekins, rolling it around the sides, with 2 slices in each ramekin.
3. Line the inside of each ramekin with a slice of ham. Crack one egg into each of them. Flavour it with salt plus pepper
4. Place the ramekins into the cooking basket and cook for 15 minutes at 160ºC. Serve.

Nutrition: Calories 82; Fat 5g; Carbs 17g; Protein 5g

French Toast Slices

Preparation time: 10 minutes
Cooking time: 10 minutes
Servings: 2

Ingredients:
- 5 slices of sandwich bread, cut into 3 equal pieces
- 2 eggs
- 100ml milk

- 2 tbsp flour
- 3 tbsp sugar
- 1 tsp ground cinnamon
- half tsp of vanilla extract
- Pinch of salt

Directions:
1. Preheat your air fryer to 220ºC.
2. Combine the eggs, milk, flour, sugar, ground cinnamon, vanilla extract, and salt in your bowl until smooth. Dip the bread slices into the mixture until well coated.
3. Arrange a parchment paper inside your air fryer, and add the bread in one layer. Cook within 5 minutes, flip the bread and cook within 5 minutes. Let it cool, and serve.

Nutrition: Calories 332; Fat 3g; Carbs 24g; Protein 6g

Loaded Hash Browns

Preparation time: 10 minutes + soaking time
Cooking time: 20 minutes
Servings: 4
Ingredients:
- 3 potatoes, grated & squeezed the excess water
- 1 green pepper, chopped
- 1 red pepper, chopped
- 1 small onion, chopped
- 2 cloves of garlic, chopped
- 1 tsp paprika
- 2 tsp olive oil
- Pinch of salt
- Pinch of pepper

Directions:

1. Place your potatoes in your large bowl with cold water and soak for 25 minutes. Drain and dry it well.
2. Transfer the potatoes to your large bowl, add the spices and oil, and then mix them well.
3. Add your potatoes to your fryer basket and cook for 10 minutes at 200ºC. Open the lid and shake your air fryer basket.
4. Put the onions and peppers, then cook within 10 minutes. Serve.

Nutrition: Calories 246; Fat 3g; Carbs 42g; Protein 6g

Breakfast Eggs & Spinach

Preparation time: 10 minutes
Cooking time: 15-20 minutes
Servings: 4
Ingredients:
- 500g fresh spinach, wilted
- 200g sliced deli ham
- 1 tbsp olive oil
- 4 eggs
- 4 tsp milk
- Salt & pepper to taste
- 1 tbsp butter for cooking

Directions:
1. Preheat your air fryer to 180ºC—coat 4 small ramekins with a bit of butter.
2. Arrange the wilted spinach, ham, 1 tsp of milk, and 1 egg into each ramekin. Flavour it with salt plus pepper.
3. Transfer them to your cooking basket, and cook within 15 to 20 minutes until the egg is set. Serve.

Nutrition: Calories 162; Fat 1g; Carbs 25g; Protein 10g

German Style Pancakes

Preparation time: 10 minutes
Cooking time: 6-8 minutes
Servings: 5
Ingredients:
- 3 eggs
- 120g flour
- 250ml milk
- Pinch of salt
- 2 tbsp unsweetened applesauce

Directions:
1. Preheat your fryer to 200ºC and insert a greased ramekin inside.
2. Blend the eggs, milk, applesauce, flour, and salt in your blender until smooth.
3. Add the batter in your ramekin, and cook within 6 to 8 minutes until brown. Serve!

Nutrition: Calories 139; Fat 4g; Carbs 18g; Protein 8g

Patatas Bravas

Preparation time: 10 minutes
Cooking time: 15 minutes
Servings: 4

Ingredients:
- 300g potatoes, cut into chunks
- 1 tbsp avocado oil
- 1 tbsp smoked paprika
- 1 tsp garlic powder
- Pinch of salt
- Pinch of pepper
- Water, as needed

Directions:
1. Boil a large saucepan with enough water and cook the potatoes for 6 minutes. Strain well and pat the potatoes dry with a paper towel. Let it cool.
2. Mix the garlic powder, salt, pepper, and avocado oil in a large bowl. Mix in the potatoes until well-coated.
3. Place them in one layer in the cooking basket. Cook the potatoes for 15 minutes at 200ºC, and shake at the halfway point. Serve!

Nutrition: Calories 97; Fat 4g; Carbs 15g; Protein 1g

Blueberry & Lemon Muffins

Preparation time: 15 minutes
Cooking time: 10 minutes
Servings: 12 muffins
Ingredients:
- 315g self-raising flour
- 65g sugar
- 120ml double cream
- 2 tbsp of light cooking oil
- 2 eggs
- 125g blueberries
- Zest & juice of a lemon
- 1 tsp vanilla

Directions:
1. Mix the self-raising flour and sugar in a small bowl.
2. Mix the oil, juice, eggs, cream, and vanilla in another bowl. Mix both the prepared mixture and blueberries.
3. Spoon the mixture into the individual silicon muffin moulds, arrange them in your air fryer

basket, and cook at 150ºC for 10 minutes until brown. Serve.

Nutrition: Calories 313; Fat 7g; Carbs 54g; Protein 6g

Macaroni and Cheese Quiche

Preparation time: 10 minutes
Cooking time: 20 minutes
Servings: 4

Ingredients:
- 8 tbsp macaroni cheese, cooked
- 2 sheets of shortcrust pastry
- 2 tbsp Greek yoghurt
- 2 eggs
- 150ml milk
- 1 tsp garlic puree
- A little grated cheese to serve

Directions:
1. Flour the inside of 4 ramekins, and add the pastry.
2. Mix the yoghurt, garlic and macaroni in a bowl. Add the mixture into the ramekins until ¾ full.
3. Whisk the milk plus egg in your small bowl, then pour it on the macaroni. Sprinkle the cheese on top.
4. Preheat your air fryer to 180ºC and cook the quiche for 20 minutes until golden brown. Serve.

Nutrition: Calories 191; Fat 8g; Carbs 18g; Protein 10g

Air Fried Sausage

Preparation time: 5 minutes
Cooking time: 10 minutes
Servings: 4
Ingredients:
- 4 links of sausages, uncooked

Directions:
1. Place a parchment paper in your cooking basket. Arrange the sausages inside with a little space between them.
2. Cook them at 180ºC within 15 minutes, flip and cook again within 5 minutes. Serve.

Nutrition: Calories 260; Fat 21g; Carbs 3g; Protein 14g

Radish Hash Browns

Preparation time: 10 minutes
Cooking time: 13 minutes
Servings: 4
Ingredients:
- 250g radish, trim off the roots
- 1 chopped onion
- 1 tsp onion powder
- .75 tsp sea salt

- .50 tsp paprika
- .25 tsp black pepper
- 1 tsp coconut oil

Directions:
1. Process the radish in your food processor until grated. Add the onions and process again until chopped.
2. Add the coconut oil and mix it well. Transfer this mixture to the air fryer basket and cook at 180ºC within 8 minutes, shaking the basket a few times.
3. Transfer the mixture into a bowl, season it with onion powder, salt, paprika, and pepper, and then mix it well.
4. Place the mixture back into your air fryer basket, and cook at 200ºC within 5 minutes until golden brown. Serve.

Nutrition: Calories 486; Fat 26g; Carbs 25g; Protein 25g

Cooking time: 5 minutes
Servings: 4

Ingredients:
- 1 packet of Pillsbury Grands or any packaged pizza-style dough
- 5 tbsp raspberry jam
- 1 tbsp melted butter
- 5 tbsp sugar

Directions:
1. Warm up your air fryer to 250ºC.
2. Place the dough into your cooking basket and cook within 5 minutes. Let it cool.
3. Coat the doughnuts with butter. Add the sugar to a large bowl, and dip the doughnut until well coated.
4. Place the jam into an icing bag and pipe it into each doughnut. Serve.

Nutrition: Calories 546; Fat 6g; Carbs 34g; Protein 22g

Breakfast Doughnuts

Preparation time: 10 minutes

POULTRY RECIPES

Barbecue Chicken Thighs

Preparation time: 5 minutes
Cooking time: 30 minutes
Servings: 3
Ingredients:
- 6 chicken thighs with skin on
- 5ml oil
- 14g of plain flour
- 14g of barbecue seasoning

Directions:
1. Preheat your air fryer to 180°C. Spray the chicken thighs with the oil
2. Combine the BBQ seasoning plus flour in your small bowl. Rub this mixture into the chicken thighs.
3. Arrange them in your cooking basket and cook for 30 minutes, turning halfway. Serve.

Nutrition: Calories 250; Fat 21g; Carbs 5g; Protein 30g

Tandoori Chicken

Preparation time: 10 minutes
Cooking time: 20 minutes
Servings: 2
Ingredients:
- 500g halved chicken tenders
- 75g Greek yoghurt
- 1 tbsp minced ginger
- 1 tbsp minced garlic
- 1 tsp paprika
- 1 tsp salt
- 1 tsp cayenne
- 1 tsp garam masala
- 1 tsp turmeric
- 8g chopped cilantro
- Cooking oil, as needed

Directions:
1. Mix the yoghurt, ginger, garlic, paprika, salt, cayenne, garam masala, turmeric, and cilantro in a large bowl.
2. Warm up your air fryer to 160ºC. Place the chicken in your cooking basket and grease it with oil.
3. Cook within 10 minutes, flip, and cook again within 5 minutes. Pour the prepared sauce on top and cook within 5 minutes. Serve!

Nutrition: Calories 178; Fat 6g; Carbs 2g; Protein 25g

Bacon Wrapped Chicken Thighs

Preparation time: 10 minutes
Cooking time: 20 minutes
Servings: 4
Ingredients:
- 5 chicken thighs, no skin or bones
- 150g butter, softened
- 1 garlic clove, minced
- .25 tsp dried thyme

- .25 tsp dried basil
- A pinch of salt
- A pinch of pepper
- 5 rashers of bacon

Directions:
1. Mix the butter, garlic, thyme, basil, salt and pepper in your bowl. Place the butter onto the cling film and roll it up. Keep it within 2 hours in your fridge until firm.
2. Open the butter and place one strip of bacon on top to coat a little. Add the chicken thighs and sprinkle a little extra garlic.
3. Add a little butter to the middle of the chicken thigh and tuck the end of the bacon inside the chicken to secure it.
4. Preheat the air fryer to 180ºC. Arrange the chicken inside your cooking basket, and cook for 20 minutes until golden brown. Serve.

Nutrition: Calories 453; Fat 34g; Carbs 33g; Protein 15g

Chicken Goujons

Preparation time: 10 minutes
Cooking time: 15 minutes
Servings: 4
Ingredients:
- 500g chicken breast meat, cut into 5/6 cm strips
- 60g mayonnaise
- 20g mustard
- 30ml full-fat milk
- 40g bacon powder
- 5ml oil

Directions:
1. Preheat your air fryer to 200ºC. Line the air fryer tray with foil and spray with oil.
2. Mix the mayonnaise, mustard and milk in a bowl. Rub this mixture into the chicken and coat them with the bacon powder.
3. Arrange the chicken goujons into the cooking basket and cook within 15 minutes. Serve.

Nutrition: Calories 170; Fat 9g; Carbs 0g; Protein 8g

Buffalo Chicken Casserole

Preparation time: 10 minutes
Cooking time: 18 minutes
Servings: 4
Ingredients:
- 500g rotisserie chicken, shredded
- 58g chopped onion
- 36g cream
- 59ml hot wing sauce
- 60g blue cheese, crumbled
- 64g cream cheese, diced
- Salt & black pepper to taste
- 3g spring onion, chopped

Directions:
1. Preheat the air fryer to 176°C, line it using parchment paper, and grease it with cooking spray.
2. Mix the rotisserie chicken, onion, cream, hot wing sauce, blue cheese, cream cheese, salt and black pepper in a bowl.
3. Transfer the chicken mixture to the cooking basket, and cook for 15 minutes. Remove the basket, cover it with foil, and cook for 3 minutes.
4. Garnish the chicken casserole with spring onion, and serve.

Nutrition: Calories 348; Fat 22g; Carbs 3g; Protein 34g

Crunchy Chicken Tenders

Preparation time: 15 minutes
Cooking time: 12 minutes
Servings: 2

Ingredients:
- 1 egg
- 1 tbsp olive oil
- 25g dry breadcrumbs
- 4 frozen chicken tenders

Directions:
1. Preheat the fryer to 175ºC.
2. Beat the egg in a small bowl. Mix the breadcrumbs plus oil in the second bowl. Dip one chicken tender into the egg, then into the breadcrumbs. Repeat with the remaining tenders.
3. Add them in your basket, and cook for 12 minutes. Serve!

Nutrition: Calories 253; Fat 11g; Carbs 9g; Protein 26g

Chicken Fajitas

Preparation time: 10 minutes
Cooking time: 18 minutes
Servings: 4

Ingredients:
- 2 sliced bell peppers
- 1 sliced onion
- 450g chicken breast, sliced into strips
- 20g of fajita seasoning
- 5-10ml cooking oil

Directions:
1. Preheat your air fryer to 180°C.
2. Coat the sliced chicken and vegetables with the fajita seasoning in a bowl, then spray it with the oil.
3. Arrange the mixture into a cooking basket, and cook within 18 minutes. Serve.

Nutrition: Calories 235; Fat 2g; Carbs 2g; Protein 10g

Pepper & Lemon Chicken Wings

Preparation time: 10 minutes
Cooking time: 26 minutes
Servings: 2

Ingredients:
- 1kg chicken wings
- 1/4 tsp cayenne pepper
- 2 tsp lemon pepper seasoning
- 3 tbsp butter, melted
- 1 tsp honey
- An extra 1 tsp lemon pepper seasoning for the sauce

Directions:
1. Preheat the air fryer to 260ºC.
2. Mix the lemon pepper seasoning and cayenne in a bowl. Mix in the wings until coated.
3. Arrange them in your cooking basket and cook for 20 minutes, turning halfway. Adjust to 300ºC and cook for another 6 minutes.
4. Meanwhile, mix the butter, honey and remaining seasoning. Remove the wings and pour the honey sauce on top. Serve.

Nutrition: Calories 356; Fat 6g; Carbs 31g; Protein 8g

Cheesy Chicken Chimichangas

Preparation time: 15 minutes
Cooking time: 7 minutes
Servings: 6

Ingredients:
- 6 large tortillas
- 2 chicken breasts, cooked and shredded
- 4 tbsp mild salsa
- .25 tsp black pepper
- 30g refried beans
- 1 jalapeno pepper, chopped
- 1 tsp cumin
- .50 tsp chilli powder
- .25 tsp salt

Directions:
1. Mix the chicken breasts, refried beans, salsa, jalapeno, pepper, cumin, chilli powder, and salt in a large bowl.
2. Add a third of the mixture in one tortilla, and roll it like a burrito to secure the filling.
3. Grease your cooking basket and warm up your air fryer to 200ºC.
4. Arrange the filled wraps into the cooking basket and cook for 7 minutes. Serve hot.

Nutrition: Calories 486; Fat 26g; Carbs 25g; Protein 25g

Spicy Chicken Wings

Preparation time: 15 minutes
Cooking time: 25 minutes
Servings: 4
Ingredients:
- 1kg chicken wings, trim off the tips
- 14g of garam masala seasoning
- 5–10ml oil

Directions:
1. Preheat your air fryer to 180°C.
2. Coat the chicken wings with the oil and garam masala. Add the spicy wings in your basket and cook for 20–25 minutes, shaking them every 5 minutes. Serve.

Nutrition: Calories 206; Fat 15g; Carbs 1g; Protein 18g

Olive-Stained Turkey Breast

Preparation time: 10 minutes + marinating time
Cooking time: 15 minutes
Servings: 4
Ingredients:
- The brine from a can of olives
- 150ml buttermilk
- 300g boneless and skinless turkey breasts
- 1 sprig of fresh rosemary
- 2 sprigs of fresh thyme

Directions:
1. Mix the olive brine and buttermilk in a bowl. Pour this mixture over the turkey breast, and add the rosemary and thyme sprigs.
2. Place into the fridge for 8 hours to marinate. Remove and let the turkey reach room temperature.
3. Preheat the air fryer to 175°C. Add the turkey breast in your cooking basket, and cook for 15 minutes until brown. Serve.

Nutrition: Calories 234; Fat 21g; Carbs 41g; Protein 12g

Turkey Melt Sandwich

Preparation time: 10 minutes
Cooking time: 15 minutes
Servings: 4

Ingredients:
- 4 slices lean turkey
- 8 slices whole-wheat bread
- 8 slices of tomato
- 4 slices of cheese

Directions:
1. Preheat the air fryer to 180°C.
2. Top each bread slice with cheese, turkey and tomato slices. Press two slices of bread together to make a sandwich.
3. Add the turkey sandwiches inside your air fryer basket and cook within 15 minutes. Serve.

Nutrition: Calories 294; Fat 15g; Carbs 25g; Protein 16g

Turkey and Mushroom Burgers

Preparation time: 10 minutes
Cooking time: 10 minutes
Servings: 2
Ingredients:
- 180g mushrooms
- 500g minced turkey
- 1 tsp garlic powder
- 1 tsp onion powder
- .50 tsp salt
- .50 tsp pepper

Directions:
1. Process the mushrooms in your food processor until pureed. Season it with garlic & onion powder, salt, plus pepper, then process once more.
2. Transfer it into a bowl, add the turkey and mix it well. Form the burger using this mixture.

3. Spray each burger with cooking spray, arrange them in the cooking basket, and cook at 160°C for 10 minutes, flipping after 5 minutes. Serve.

Nutrition: Calories 132; Fat 26g; Carbs 25g; Protein 25g

Turkey Cutlets with Mushroom Sauce

Preparation time: 15 minutes
Cooking time: 21 minutes
Servings: 4
Ingredients:
- 4 turkey cutlets
- 2 tbsp butter
- 1 can of cream of mushroom sauce
- 160ml milk
- Salt & pepper, as needed

Directions:
1. Preheat the air fryer to 220°C.
2. Brush the turkey cutlets with butter, salt, and pepper. Add the

cutlets in your basket, and cook within 11 minutes.

3. Add the mushroom soup and milk to a pan, then cook for 10 minutes over medium heat, stirring until thickened. Top this mixture on the turkey cutlets. Serve!

Nutrition: Calories 426; Fat 21g; Carbs 18g; Protein 16g

Turkey Stuffed Peppers

Preparation time: 15 minutes
Cooking time: 13-15 minutes
Servings: 3
Ingredients:
- 3 red bell pepper, cut off the tops & deseeded
- 1 tbsp olive oil
- 347g ground turkey
- 68g brown rice, cooked
- 27g bread crumbs
- 180g low-sodium marinara sauce
- 3 tbsp finely chopped parsley
- .25 tbsp ground pepper
- 13g parmesan cheese, grated
- 56g part-skim mozzarella cheese, shredded
- Cooking spray
- Parsley for garnishing

Directions:
1. Warm up your air fryer to 176°C and grease the cooking basket.
2. Heat the oil in your skillet oil over medium heat, and cook the turkey within 4 minutes. Add the rice and bread crumbs, then cook within 1 minute. Set aside.
3. Stir in the marinara, parsley, pepper, and parmesan to the turkey mixture. Divide this mixture among the bell pepper, and cover it with the reserved pepper tops.
4. Add the peppers in your cooking basket, and cook within 8 minutes. Remove the pepper tops and sprinkle them with the mozzarella.
5. Cook again for 2 minutes; sprinkle it with parsley before serving.

Nutrition: Calories 407; Fat 21g; Carbs 26g; Protein 29g

BEEF, PORK AND LAMB RECIPES

Beef Wellington

Preparation time: 10 minutes
Cooking time: 35 minutes
Servings: 4

Ingredients:
- 1kg beef fillet (one large piece)
- 2 sheets of shortcrust pastry
- 1 egg, beaten
- Chicken pate, as needed
- Salt & pepper to taste

Directions:
1. Flavour the beef with salt and pepper, then wrap it tightly in a cling film. Let it chill in your fridge within hour.
2. Roll out the pastry and brush the sides with the egg. Spread the chicken pate on top, making sure it is distributed equally.
3. Remove the cling film, then arrange the beef in the middle of the pastry. Wrap the pastry around the beef and seal the edges with a fork.
4. Place it in your basket and cook at 160ºC within 35 minutes. Serve.

Nutrition: Calories 400; Fat 26g; Carbs 19g; Protein 20g

Italian Meatballs

Preparation time: 15 minutes
Cooking time: 12-14 minutes
Servings: 4
Ingredients:
- 500g minced beef
- 25g grated Parmesan cheese
- 80g breadcrumbs
- 10g onion powder
- 2g Italian seasoning
- 10g dried parsley
- 1 egg
- 30ml milk
- 5–10ml oil
- Salt & pepper to taste

Directions:
1. Preheat your air fryer to 190°C.
2. Mix the Parmesan cheese, breadcrumbs, onion powder, Italian seasoning, dried parsley, salt, and pepper in a bowl.
3. Add the minced beef, beaten egg, and milk, then mix it well. Divide the mixture into 16 meatballs of equal size and spray with the oil.
4. Place the meatballs in the cooking basket in one layer, and cook for 12 to 14 minutes. Serve.

Nutrition: Calories 150; Fat 8g; Carbs 2g; Protein 8g

Beef Broccoli Stir-Fry

Preparation time: 10 minutes + marinating time
Cooking time: 11 minutes
Servings: 2

Ingredients:
- 500g beef steak
- 500g broccoli
- 3 peppers, cut into strips
- 1 tbsp ground ginger
- .25 cup water
- 1 onion, sliced
- .25 cup hoisin sauce
- 1 tsp sesame oil + 1 tbsp
- 2 tsp garlic minced
- 1 tbsp soy sauce

Directions:
1. Mix the sesame oil, hoisin sauce, garlic, soy and water in a large bowl. Mix in the steak and marinate within 20 minutes.
2. Mix 1 tbsp of oil with the broccoli and peppers. Place them into the cooking basket and cook at 200ºC for 5 minutes. Move it to your bowl.

3. Add the marinated steak to the cooking basket and cook for 4 minutes. Flip, and cook again within 2 minutes. Mix the steak with the vegetables, then serve.

Nutrition: Calories 359; Fat 32g; Carbs 18g; Protein 25g

Bulgogi Beef Burgers

Preparation time: 10 minutes + chilling time
Cooking time: 10 minutes
Servings: 4
Ingredients:
- 500g minced beef
- 2 tbsp gochujang
- 1 tbsp soy
- 2 tsp garlic, minced
- 2 tsp ginger, minced
- 1 onion, chopped
- 1 tbsp olive oil
- 2 tsp sugar
- Burger buns, as needed

Directions:
1. Mix the gochujang, soy, garlic, ginger, onion, olive oil, and sugar in a large bowl. Put it in your fridge within 30 minutes.
2. Form the burgers from the minced beef, and add the burgers in your cooking basket. Cook for 10 minutes at 180ºC.
3. Serve it in a burger bun with the prepared mixture on top.

Nutrition: Calories 392; Fat 29g; Carbs 7g; Protein 24g

Beef Fried Rice

Preparation time: 15 minutes
Cooking time: 20 minutes
Servings: 2

Ingredients:
- 100g cooked rice
- 500g beef strips, cooked
- 1 tbsp sesame oil
- 1 onion, diced
- 1 egg
- 2 tsp garlic powder
- 1 tbsp vegetable oil
- 100g frozen peas
- Salt & pepper to taste

Directions:
1. Warm up air fryer to 175ºC.
2. Flavour the beef with garlic powder, salt, plus pepper. Cook it in your pan over medium heat for 5 minutes until almost done
3. Mix the rice with peas, carrots and oil. Pour it to the beef and mix it well.
4. Add the beef fried rice to your cooking basket and cook within 10 minutes. Add the egg and cook for 5 minutes until the egg has set. Serve.

Nutrition: Calories 250; Fat 26g; Carbs 36g; Protein 19g

Roast Pork Loin

Preparation time: 15 minutes
Cooking time: 50 minutes
Servings: 6

Ingredients:
- 1kg pork loin joint with the rind on; score the rind with a sharp knife (making 3–4 deep cuts)
- 4g sea salt
- 2 grated garlic cloves
- 4g dried mixed herbs
- 5ml oil

Directions:
1. Preheat your air fryer to 180°C.
2. Mix the salt, garlic and mixed herbs in a small bowl. Rub this mixture into the pork rind until well coated, and spray it with oil.
3. Place the pork in the cooking basket and cook for 50 minutes, shaking the basket every 5 minutes. Let it cool, and serve.
4. Remove the pork from the fryer and rest for 10 minutes

Nutrition: Calories 220; Fat 6g; Carbs 0g; Protein 10g

Garlic Pork Chops with Courgette

Preparation time: 15 minutes + marinating time
Cooking time: 20 minutes
Servings: 4

Ingredients:
- 1 thinly sliced courgette
- 250g asparagus
- 4 pork chops
- 30g garlic powder
- 10g dried oregano
- 30ml oil
- Juice of one lemon
- Salt & pepper to taste

Directions:
1. Mix the oil, lemon juice, oregano, and garlic powder in a bowl. Add the chops, and mix until well-coated. Cover, and keep in your fridge to marinate for 1 hour.
2. Preheat your air fryer to 200°C. Spray the air fryer basket with the oil and line it with parchment.
3. Place the chops on the air fryer basket and pour any remaining marinade. Arrange the sliced courgette and asparagus around the chops.
4. Cook for 20 minutes, turning halfway. Let it cool, and serve.

Nutrition: Calories 210; Fat 9g; Carbs 2g; Protein 20g

Pork Schnitzel

Preparation time: 10 minutes
Cooking time: 20 minutes
Servings: 2

Ingredients:
- 3 pork steaks, cubed
- Salt & pepper to taste
- 75g plain flour
- 2 eggs
- 125g breadcrumbs

Directions:
1. Flavour the pork with salt and pepper. Coat the pork in the flour, then dip it into the egg. Lastly, coat it in breadcrumbs.
2. Arrange them in the air fryer basket and cook at 175ºC for 20 minutes, turning halfway. Serve.

Nutrition: Calories 467; Fat 32g; Carbs 27g; Protein 18g

Tender Ham Steaks

Preparation time: 15 minutes
Cooking time: 12 minutes
Servings: 1
Ingredients:
- 1 ham steak
- 2 tbsp brown sugar
- 1 tsp honey
- 2 tbsp melted butter

Directions:
1. Preheat the air fryer to 220ºC.
2. Whisk the butter and sugar in your bowl until smooth. Add the ham to the air fryer basket and brush it with the prepared mixture.
3. Cook for 12 minutes, turning halfway and re-brushing the ham. Drizzle the honey on top before serving.

Nutrition: Calories 419; Fat 23g; Carbs 31g; Protein 14g

Mustard Pork Tenderloin

Preparation time: 10 minutes
Cooking time: 25 minutes
Servings: 2
Ingredients:
- 1 pork tenderloin
- 3 tbsp soy sauce
- 2 minced garlic cloves
- 3 tbsp olive oil
- 2 tbsp brown sugar
- 1 tbsp Dijon mustard
- Salt & pepper to taste

Directions:
1. Mix the soy sauce, garlic, Dijon mustard, olive oil, salt, brown sugar, and pepper in your bowl. Pour it into your Ziplock bag and add the pork.
2. Knead the bag until the pork is well coated. Keep in your fridge for 30 minutes to marinate.
3. Preheat your air fryer to 260ºC. Put the marinated pork in the cooking basket.
4. Cook for 25 minutes, turning halfway. Let it rest, slice, and serve.

Nutrition: Calories 437; Fat 37g; Carbs 21g; Protein 31g

Roast Lamb Rack with Lemon Crust

Preparation time: 15 minutes
Cooking time: 30 minutes
Servings: 4
Ingredients:
- 794g rack of lamb
- Salt & black pepper to taste
- 53g breadcrumbs
- 1 tbsp garlic clove, grated
- 1 tbsp cumin seeds
- 1 tbsp ground cumin
- 1 tbsp oil
- One-fourth lemon rinds, grated
- 1 egg, beaten

Directions:
1. Preheat the air fryer to 100°C.
2. Flavour the rack of lamb with salt and pepper. Set aside.
3. Mix the bread crumbs, garlic, cumin seeds, ground cumin, oil, and lemon rinds in a bowl. Place the egg on a shallow plate.
4. Dip the lamb in your egg, then into the crumb's mixture. Put the lamb in the basket and cook for 25 minutes.
5. Adjust to 200°C and cook the lamb within 5 minutes. Serve.

Nutrition: Calories 400; Fat 24g; Carbs 4g; Protein 44g

Lamb Calzone

Preparation time: 10 minutes
Cooking time: 0 minutes
Servings: 2
Ingredients:
- 1 tsp olive oil
- 1 chopped onion
- 100g baby spinach leaves
- 400g minced pork
- 250g whole wheat pizza dough
- 300g grated cheese

Directions:
1. Heat the olive oil in your pan, and cook the onion within 2 minutes. Add the spinach and cook within 1 minute. Stir in the marinara sauce and minced pork
2. Split your dough into 4 and roll out into circles. Add one-fourth of the filling to each piece of dough.
3. Sprinkle it with cheese and fold the dough over to create half-moons; crimp edges to seal.
4. Spray the calzones with cooking spray, arrange them in the cooking basket and cook at 160°C for 12 minutes, turning after 8 minutes. Serve.

Nutrition: Calories 348; Fat 12g; Carbs 44g; Protein 21g

Lamb Burgers

Preparation time: 10 minutes
Cooking time: 18 minutes
Servings: 4

Ingredients:
- 600g minced lamb
- 2 tsp garlic puree
- 1 tsp harissa paste
- 2 tbsp Moroccan spice
- Salt & pepper to taste

Directions:
1. Mix the minced lamb, garlic puree, harissa paste, Moroccan spice, salt, and pepper in a bowl. Form it into burgers
2. Arrange them in the cooking basket and cook at 180ºC for 18 minutes. Serve.

Nutrition: Calories 423; Fat 38g; Carbs 3g; Protein 30g

Lamb Meatballs

Preparation time: 20 minutes
Cooking time: 15 minutes
Servings: 6
Ingredients:
- 454g minced lamb
- 1 tbsp ground cumin
- 2 tbsp each of granulated onion & fresh parsley
- .25 tbsp ground cinnamon
- Salt & black pepper, as needed

Directions:
1. Mix the minced lamb, cumin, onion, parsley, cinnamon, salt, and black pepper in a bowl. Form the lamb meatballs from this mixture.
2. Lightly mist the meatballs with cooking spray, and arrange them in one layer in your air fryer basket.

3. Cook the meatballs at 176ºC for 15 minutes, shaking halfway. Serve.

Nutrition: Calories 328; Fat 22g; Carbs 1g; Protein 27g

Herbed Lamb Chops

Preparation time: 10 minutes + marinating time
Cooking time: 7 minutes
Servings: 4

Ingredients:
- 454g lamb chops
- 1 tbsp rosemary
- 1 tbsp thyme
- 1 tbsp oregano
- 1 tbsp salt
- 1 tbsp coriander
- 2 tbsp olive oil
- 2 tbsp lemon juice

Directions:
1. Mix the rosemary, thyme, oregano, salt, coriander, olive oil, and lemon juice in a resealable

bag. Add the lamb chops and knead until coated. Marinate it in your fridge within 1 hour.

2. Preheat the air fryer to 198°C. Add the lamb chops in your basket and cook for 7 minutes. Flip the lamb chops after 3 minutes of cooking. Serve.

Nutrition: Calories 414; Fat 37g; Carbs 1g; Protein 19g

FISH AND SEAFOOD RECIPES

Paprika Salmon Fillets

Preparation time: 5 minutes
Cooking time: 5 minutes
Servings: 3

Ingredients:
- 3 salmon fillets
- 8g paprika seasoning
- 10ml oil

Directions:
1. Preheat your air fryer to 190°C.
2. Whisk the oil plus paprika in your bowl. Rub it onto the salmon fillets until well coated.
3. Add the fillets in your basket and cook within 5 minutes. Serve.

Nutrition: Calories 179; Fat 2g; Carbs 1g; Protein 14g

Lemon Mahi-Mahi

Preparation time: 10 minutes
Cooking time: 14 minutes
Servings: 4
Ingredients:
- 180g mahi-mahi
- 2 tbsp butter
- 6cm lemon slice
- 1 tsp white salt

Directions:
1. Place the mahi-mahi in an aluminium foil dish, and brush it with butter. Add the lemon slices on top.
2. Place the aluminium dish into the cooking basket, and cook at 175°C for 14 minutes—season with salt to taste before serving.

Nutrition: Calories 91; Fat 7g; Carbs 2g; Protein 7g

Baked Crunchy Cod

Preparation time: 10 minutes
Cooking time: 15 minutes
Servings: 5
Ingredients:
- 2 pieces of cod cut into smaller portions (around five)
- 4 tbsp of panko breadcrumbs
- 1 egg
- 1 egg white
- .50 tsp onion powder
- .50 tsp garlic salt
- A pinch of pepper
- .50 tsp mixed herbs

Directions:
1. Warm up your air fryer to 220°C.
2. Mix the onion powder, garlic salt, pepper, and herbs in another

bowl. Rub this mixture on the fish until well coated.

3. Mix the egg plus egg white in your small bowl. Dip each cod fish into the egg, then coat it in the panko breadcrumbs

4. Place a tin foil inside your air fryer basket, add the fish and cook for 15 minutes. Serve.

Nutrition: Calories 340; Fat 26g; Carbs 23g; Protein 14g

Garlic and Lemon Plaice

Preparation time: 10 minutes
Cooking time: 8-10 minutes
Servings: 2
Ingredients:
- 2 large plaice fillets
- 2 grated garlic cloves
- 10ml lemon juice
- 2g onion powder
- 4g dried parsley
- 5ml oil
- Salt & pepper to taste

Directions:

1. Preheat your air fryer to 180°C.
2. Mix the garlic, onion powder, parsley, salt, and pepper in a bowl. Flavour the fillet with this mixture, and spray it with the lemon juice.
3. Spray the air fryer basket with oil, arrange the fillets inside and cook for 8 to 10 minutes, turning halfway. Serve.

Nutrition: Calories 160; Fat 1g; Carbs 4g; Protein 15g

Tomato and Herb Tuna Steak

Preparation time: 10 minutes + marinating time
Cooking time: 7-10 minutes
Servings: 2
Ingredients:
- 2 tuna steaks
- 15ml extra virgin olive oil
- 125g cherry tomatoes
- 4g dried basil
- 2g dried thyme
- 2g dried oregano
- 5ml oil
- Salt & pepper to taste

Directions:

1. Flavour the tuna steaks with thyme, oregano, salt, half of the basil, plus pepper. Let it chill within 10 minutes in your fridge.
2. Drizzle the oil on the tomatoes and sprinkle with the remaining basil.
3. Preheat your air fryer to 190°C. Spray the inside of the cooking basket with the oil.
4. Lay the tuna steaks in the air fryer basket and arrange the tomatoes

around them. Cook for 7–10 minutes, turning the steaks halfway. Serve.

Nutrition: Calories 320; Fat 8g; Carbs 2g; Protein 20g

Tuna Fish Cakes

Preparation time: 10 minutes
Cooking time: 8 minutes
Servings: 4

Ingredients:
- 140g tinned, drained tuna
- 60g bacon powder
- 5g dried herbs
- 110g grated cheese
- 7g mayonnaise
- 1 beaten egg
- 10ml water
- 10ml oil

Directions:
1. Preheat your air fryer to 190°C.
2. Mix the tuna, bacon powder, dried herbs, cheese, mayonnaise, egg,

and water in a bowl. Form this mixture into 8 fish cakes.
3. Arrange the fish cakes in the fryer basket, and cook within 8 minutes. Serve.

Nutrition: Calories 250; Fat 6g; Carbs 1g; Protein 10g

Sriracha with Salmon

Preparation time: 10 minutes + marinating time
Cooking time: 12 minutes
Servings: 2

Ingredients:
- 3 tbsp sriracha
- 4 tbsp honey
- 1 tbsp soy sauce
- 500g salmon fillets

Directions:
1. Mix the honey, soy sauce and sriracha in a medium bowl. Add the salmon with the skin facing upwards. Let it marinate for 30 minutes.
2. Warm up your air fryer to 200°C. Spray the cooking basket with cooking spray
3. Place the salmon into the cooking basket skin side down, and cook for 12 minutes until browned. Serve!

Nutrition: Calories 320; Fat 34g; Carbs 25g; Protein 25g

Tilapia Fillets

Preparation time: 15 minutes
Cooking time: 10 minutes
Servings: 3

Ingredients:
- 50g almond flour
- 3 fillets of tilapia fish
- 2 tbsp butter, melted
- 1 tsp black pepper
- .50 tsp salt
- 4 tbsp mayonnaise
- A handful of almonds sliced thinly

Directions:
1. Mix the almond flour, butter, pepper and salt in a bowl.
2. Spread the mayonnaise on the fish, and coat it in the almond flour mixture. Spread the sliced almonds on one side of the fish.
3. Spray the air fryer with a little cooking spray. Add the fish to the cooking basket and cook at 160ºC for 10 minutes. Serve.

Nutrition: Calories 724; Fat 59g; Carbs 13g; Protein 41g

Pretzel Crusted Catfish

Preparation time: 20 minutes
Cooking time: 12 minutes
Servings: 4

Ingredients:
- 4 catfish fillets
- .50 tbsp salt
- .50 tbsp black pepper
- 2 eggs
- 5 1/3 tbsp Dijon mustard
- 2 tbsp 2% milk
- 63g all-purpose flour
- 946ml honey mustard miniature pretzel, crushed
- Cooking spray

Directions:
1. Preheat the air fryer to 162°C.
2. Flavour the catfish with salt plus pepper.
3. Mix the eggs, Dijon mustard, plus milk in your bowl. Place the flour and pretzels in different bowls.
4. Coat the catfish with flour, then into the egg mixture, and coat them with pretzels.
5. Arrange the catfish in the air fryer basket, then spray them with cooking spray—Cook the catfish fillets for 12 minutes. Serve.

Nutrition: Calories 466; Fat 14g; Carbs 44g; Protein 34g

Air Fried Fish Tacos

Preparation time: 10 minutes
Cooking time: 10 minutes
Servings: 4

Ingredients:
- 500g mahi-mahi fish
- 8 small tortillas
- 2 tsp Cajun seasoning
- 4 tbsp sour cream
- 2 tbsp mayo
- .25 tbsp cayenne
- 2 tbsp pepper sauce
- A little salt & pepper
- 1 tbsp sriracha sauce
- 2 tbsp lime juice

Directions:
1. Cut the fish into slices and season with salt
2. Mix the cayenne pepper, black pepper, and Cajun seasoning in a bowl. Sprinkle it onto the fish, and brush the pepper sauce on both sides.
3. Preheat your air fryer to 180°C and cook the fish for 10 minutes.
4. Mix the mayonnaise, sour cream, lime juice, sriracha and cayenne pepper in a medium bowl. Arrange the fish to your taco shell, and add the prepared sauce.
5. Assemble tacos the tacos and serve!

Nutrition: Calories 486; Fat 26g; Carbs 25g; Protein 25g

Lemon Prawns

Preparation time: 15 minutes
Cooking time: 6-7 minutes
Servings: 3

Ingredients:
- 350g uncooked prawns
- 10ml lemon juice
- 1 sliced lemon
- 2g garlic powder
- 15ml oil
- Salt & pepper, as needed

Directions:
1. Preheat your air fryer to 200°C.
2. Mix the prawns, lemon juice & slices, garlic powder, salt and pepper in a bowl.
3. Spay the air fryer basket with the oil, arrange the prawns inside and cook for 6 to 7 minutes, shaking the basket every few minutes. Serve.

Nutrition: Calories 190; Fat 4g; Carbs 6g; Protein 15g

Cajun-Style Shrimps

Preparation time: 10 minutes
Cooking time: 6 minutes
Servings: 6

Ingredients:
- 250g shrimp, cooked
- 14 slices of smoked sausage
- 4 cups part-boiled potatoes, halved
- 2 corn on the cobs, cut into smaller pieces
- 1 onion, diced
- 2 tbsp bay seasoning

Directions:
1. Mix the shrimp, sausage, potatoes, corn, onion, and bay seasoning in a bowl

2. Line the air fryer with foil. Place half the mixture into the cooking basket and cook at 200ºC for 6 minutes. Mix it well and cook for 6 minutes. Serve.

Nutrition: Calories 340; Fat 26g; Carbs 22g; Protein 30g

Garlic Caper Scallops

Preparation time: 10 minutes
Cooking time: 6 minutes
Servings: 2

Ingredients:
- 8 cleaned and dried jumbo scallops
- 50ml olive oil
- 30g dried parsley
- 1 grated clove of garlic
- 8g finely chopped capers
- 1 lemon, sliced
- Salt & pepper to taste

Directions:
1. Preheat your air fryer to 200°C.
2. Spray the scallops with the oil, arrange them in the cooking basket and cook for 4 minutes, shaking the basket halfway.
3. Mix the parsley, garlic, capers, lemons, salt, and pepper in a bowl, then toss the scallops until coated
4. Put the scallops in your cooking basket and cook for another 2 minutes. Serve.

Nutrition: Calories 250; Fat 6g; Carbs 2g; Protein 12g

Peppery Lemon Shrimp

Preparation time: 15 minutes
Cooking time: 6-8 minutes
Servings: 2
Ingredients:
- 350g prepared shrimp, uncooked
- 1 lemon, sliced
- Juice of 1 lemon
- 1 tbsp olive oil
- 1 tsp pepper
- .25 tsp paprika
- .25 tsp garlic powder

Directions:
1. Preheat the air fryer to 200ºC.
2. Mix the lemon juice, pepper, paprika, garlic powder, and olive oil in your bowl. Add the shrimp and toss it until well-coated.
3. Arrange the shrimp into the cooking basket, and cook for 6 to 8 minutes until firm. Serve!

Nutrition: Calories 215; Fat 8g; Carbs 12g; Protein 28g

Lobster Tails

Preparation time: 15 minutes
Cooking time: 6 minutes
Servings: 4

Ingredients:
- 4 lobster tails, cut it through the tail & shell pulled back
- 2 tbsp melted butter
- .50 tsp salt
- 1 tsp pepper

Directions:
1. Brush the lobster tails with melted butter, and flavour it with salt and pepper.
2. Heat the air fryer to 200ºC, arrange the lobster in your cooking basket, and cook for 4 minutes. Brush it with melted butter and cook for a further 2 minutes. Serve.

Nutrition: Calories 486; Fat 26g; Carbs 25g; Protein 25g

SIDES RECIPES

Crispy Roast Potatoes

Preparation time: 5 minutes
Cooking time: 30 minutes
Servings: 2
Ingredients:
- 2 large potatoes, peeled, chopped, parboiled & drained
- 5ml oil

Directions:
1. Preheat your air fryer to 180°C.
2. Pat the potato pieces dry and spray with the oil. Arrange them in the cooking basket and cook for 30 minutes, shaking them every 5 minutes.

Nutrition: Calories 220; Fat 3g; Carbs 26g; Protein 3g

Air Fried Green Beans

Preparation time: 10 minutes
Cooking time: 12 minutes
Servings: 4

Ingredients:
- 355g fresh green bean beans, trimmed
- 1 tbsp sesame oil
- 1 tbsp soy sauce
- 1 tbsp rice wine vinegar
- 1 garlic clove, minced
- .50 tbsp red pepper flakes

Directions:
1. Preheat the air fryer to 204°C.
2. Mix the green bean beans with the remaining in your bowl. Let it marinate for 5 minutes.
3. Transfer the green beans to the cooking basket and cook for 12 minutes. Serve.

Nutrition: Calories 60; Fat 4g; Carbs 7g; Protein 2g

Tangy Roasted Cauliflower

Preparation time: 5 minutes
Cooking time: 15 minutes
Servings: 4

Ingredients:

- 2 cauliflowers broken into florets
- 30ml sesame oil
- 2 grated cloves of garlic
- 4g paprika powder
- 5ml oil
- Salt & pepper to taste

Directions:
1. Preheat your air fryer to 200°C.
2. Mix the oil, garlic, paprika and seasoning in a bowl. Rub the mixture into the florets and spray with the oil.
3. Arrange the florets in your basket, and cook for 15 minutes. Serve.

Nutrition: Calories 60; Fat 2g; Carbs 6g; Protein 3g

Air Fried Butternut Squash

Preparation time: 10 minutes
Cooking time: 20 minutes
Servings: 6
Ingredients:
- 2 butternut squash, chopped into cubes
- 2 tbsp extra virgin oil
- 1 tbsp maple syrup
- 1 tbsp dried oregano
- .50 tbsp garlic powder
- .50 tbsp smoked paprika
- .50 tbsp salt
- .25 tbsp ground chipotle chilli pepper

Directions:
1. Mix the squash, oil, maple syrup, oregano, garlic powder, smoked paprika, salt, and chilli pepper in a large bowl.

2. Arrange the squash in your air fryer basket in one layer, and cook at 204°C for 20 minutes. Serve.

Nutrition: Calories 139; Fat 7g; Carbs 21g; Protein 2g

Crispy Brussels Sprouts

Preparation time: 10 minutes
Cooking time: 15 minutes
Servings: 4
Ingredients:
- 450g trimmed and halved Brussels sprouts
- 2g salt
- 3 finely chopped spring onions
- 28g melted butter
- 5ml white wine vinegar
- 5–10 ml oil

Directions:
1. Preheat your air fryer to 190°C.
2. Spray the sprouts with the oil and season with salt until coated.
3. Put the sprouts in your cooking basket and cook within 15 minutes.

4. Mix the spring onion, butter and white wine vinegar in a bowl. Pour it over the sprouts just before serving.

Nutrition: Calories 135; Fat 8g; Carbs 5g; Protein 4g

Stuffed Baby Artichokes

Preparation time: 15 minutes
Cooking time: 15 minutes
Servings: 10 stuffed artichokes

Ingredients:
- 907g baby artichokes, cut the stems leaving ½ cm long, remove the outer petals & cut them into halves
- 946ml of water
- 59ml lemon juice
- 225g cream cheese
- 22.50g spinach, frozen
- 8 garlic cloves, minced
- 2 tbsp olive oil
- .50 tbsp sea salt
- .25 tbsp black pepper
- 50g parmesan cheese, grated

Directions:
1. Whisk the water plus lemon juice in your bowl. Mix in the artichokes, and set aside.
2. Mash the cream cheese, spinach, and garlic in a large bowl.
3. Remove the artichokes and dry them with a paper towel. Mix it with oil, salt, plus pepper until coated.
4. Spread the spinach mixture on each artichoke, then sprinkle them with parmesan.

5. Arrange the artichokes in your cooking basket and cook them at 203°C for 15 minutes. Serve.

Nutrition: Calories 176; Fat 12g; Carbs 13g; Protein 7g

Buffalo Cauliflower

Preparation time: 15 minutes
Cooking time: 12 minutes
Servings: 8

Ingredients:
- 4kg cauliflower head, cut into florets
- 100ml cayenne pepper sauce
- 2 tbsp butter, melted
- 2 tbsp vinegar
- garlic powder to taste

Directions:
1. Preheat the air fryer to 204°C.
2. Mix the cauliflower, cayenne pepper sauce, butter, vinegar, and garlic powder in a bowl until well combined.

3. Transfer the cauliflower to the cooking basket and cook for 12 minutes. Serve.

Nutrition: Calories 228; Fat 20g; Carbs 11g; Protein 4g

Air Fried Rice

Preparation time: 15 minutes
Cooking time: 16 minutes
Servings: 2
Ingredients:
- 2 tbsp soy sauce
- 2 tbsp sriracha sauce
- 500g cooked rice
- 1 tbsp sesame oil
- 1 tbsp water
- 2 tbsp vegetable oil
- Salt & black pepper to taste
- 1 egg, beaten
- 130g peas and carrot

Directions:
1. Preheat the air fryer to 175°C.
2. Whisk the soy sauce and sriracha sauce in a bowl. Set aside.
3. Mix all the oils, rice, and water in a separate bowl. Flavour it with salt and pepper.
4. Transfer the rice mixture to a cake pan and place it in the cooking basket.
5. Cook the rice for 10 minutes, stirring halfway. Add the egg and cook within 4 minutes.
6. Stir in the peas and carrots to the rice, then cook for 2 minutes. Serve the rice with the sauce on top. Serve.

Nutrition: Calories 392; Fat 15g; Carbs 55g; Protein 11g

Garlic & Parsley Potatoes

Preparation time: 5 minutes
Cooking time: 25 minutes
Servings: 3

Ingredients:
- 500g baby potatoes, quartered
- 1 tbsp oil
- 1 tsp salt
- .50 tsp garlic powder
- .50 tsp dried parsley

Directions:
1. Preheat the air fryer to 175ºC.
2. Combine the potatoes plus oil in your bowl. Add salt, garlic powder, and dried parsley, then mix it well.
3. Transfer the potatoes to the cooking basket and cook within 25 minutes. Serve.

Nutrition: Calories 89; Fat 0g; Carbs 20g; Protein 2g

Roasted Tomatoes with Basil

Preparation time: 5 minutes
Cooking time: 10 minutes
Servings: 2
Ingredients:

- 4 medium tomatoes, halved
- 8 cherry tomatoes
- 4g dried basil
- Salt & pepper to taste
- 5–10ml oil

Directions:

1. Preheat your air fryer to 180°C.
2. Sprinkle half the basil and seasoning and spray with oil over the tomatoes until well coated.
3. Arrange them in the cooking basket and cook for 10 minutes, turning halfway. Serve.

Nutrition: Calories 30; Fat 1g; Carbs 3g; Protein 2g

Corn on the Cob

Preparation time: 5 minutes
Cooking time: 15 minutes
Servings: 4

Ingredients:

- 2 corn cobs, remove the husk and cut each cob into 2 pieces widthways
- 5–10ml oil

Directions:

1. Preheat your air fryer to 180°C.
2. Arrange the cobs in the cooking basket and spray them with the oil. Cook for 15 minutes, and serve.

Nutrition: Calories 15; Fat 0g; Carbs 1g; Protein 0g

Rosemary Roasted Vegetables

Preparation time: 10 minutes
Cooking time: 0 minutes
Servings: 4

Ingredients:

- 1 yellow pepper, sliced
- 1 red pepper, sliced
- 1 courgette, sliced
- 1 onion, sliced
- 1 broccoli head, cut into florets
- 1 tsp dried rosemary
- Salt & pepper to taste
- 10ml oil

Directions:

1. Preheat your air fryer to 180°C.
2. Toss the vegetables with the dried rosemary and oil. Season it with salt and pepper.
3. Add the vegetables in your cooking basket, and cook for 10 to 15 minutes. Serve.

Nutrition: Calories 70; Fat 1g; Carbs 2g; Protein 1g

Easy Potato Wedges

Preparation time: 10 minutes
Cooking time: 18 minutes
Servings: 4
Ingredients:
- 2 potatoes with skins on, sliced into wedges
- 1.50 tbsp olive oil
- .50 tsp paprika
- ground black pepper to taste
- .50 tsp parsley
- .50 tsp chilli powder
- .50 tsp salt

Directions:
1. Preheat the air fryer to 200ºC.
2. Mix the potatoes, olive oil, paprika, pepper, parsley, chilli powder, and salt in a bowl.
3. Add the potato wedges into your cooking basket and cook within 10 minutes. Turn and cook within 8 minutes. Serve.

Nutrition: Calories 120; Fat 5g; Carbs 19g; Protein 2g

Roasted Asparagus

Preparation time: 10 minutes
Cooking time: 5 minutes
Servings: 2

Ingredients:
- 250g asparagus, cut into small pieces
- 1 stalks of spring onion, chopped
- 2 tbsp olive oil
- .50 tbsp dried dill
- .50 tbsp salt
- .50 tbsp black pepper

Directions:
1. Toss the asparagus, spring onion, and 2 tbsp olive oil in a bowl. Season it with salt and pepper.
2. Transfer them to your cooking basket, and cook at 176°C for 5 minutes. Serve and enjoy.

Nutrition: Calories 449; Fat 14g; Carbs 73g; Protein 12g

Air Fried Cherry Tomatoes

Preparation time: 5 minutes
Cooking time: 5 minutes
Servings: 2
Ingredients:
- 250g cherry tomatoes
- 1 tbsp olive oil
- .50 tbsp salt
- .25 tbsp black pepper

Directions:
1. Mix the cherry tomatoes, olive oil, salt, plus pepper in a bowl.
2. Transfer the tomatoes to your air fryer basket, and cook at 149°C for 5 minutes. Serve.

Nutrition: Calories 133; Fat 7g; Carbs 19g; Protein 1g

VEGAN RECIPES

Sweet and Sour Tofu

Preparation time: 10 minutes
Cooking time: 20 minutes
Servings: 4

Ingredients:
- 400g cubed tofu, drained & dried
- 50ml fresh orange juice
- 16ml honey
- 5ml rice vinegar
- 2g cornflour
- 30ml soy sauce
- 14 toasted sesame seeds
- 4 chopped spring onions
- 15ml oil
- Salt & pepper to taste
- 115g brown rice, cooked

Directions:
1. Preheat your air fryer to 170°C.
2. Spray the tofu with the oil, arrange them in the cooking basket and cook for 10 minutes.
3. Meanwhile, mix the orange juice, honey, rice vinegar, cornflour, soy sauce, sesame seeds, and spring onions in a saucepan and stir over medium heat until the sauce thickens.
4. Stir the tofu into the sauce and serve with the brown rice.

Nutrition: Calories 189; Fat 5g; Carbs 12g; Protein 5g

Black Bean Patties

Preparation time: 20 minutes
Cooking time: 15 minutes
Servings: 4

Ingredients:
- 1 (400g) can of black beans, drained
- 280g rolled oats, ground
- 1 small can of sweetcorn, drained
- 2g garlic powder
- 1g chilli powder
- 15ml soy sauce
- 180ml salsa sauce
- 5ml oil

Directions:
1. Mix the black beans, oats, sweetcorn, garlic powder, chilli powder, soy sauce, and salsa sauce in a bowl. Cover and keep it in your fridge for at least 15 minutes.

2. Preheat your air fryer to 180°C. Form the prepared mixture into burgers.
3. Grease your cooking basket and line it with parchment. Make sure there are holes in the parchment for the air to circulate.
4. Arrange the patties in your basket and cook within 15 minutes. Serve.

Nutrition: Calories 170; Fat 1g; Carbs 25g; Protein 8g

Zingy Roasted Carrots

Preparation time: 5 minutes
Cooking time: 15 minutes
Servings: 2

Ingredients:
- 250g carrots, peeled & cut into chunks
- .50 tsp olive oil
- .50 tsp cayenne pepper
- Salt & pepper to taste

Directions:
1. Preheat your air fryer to 220ºC.
2. Mix the carrots, olive oil and cayenne in a bowl.
3. Arrange them in the cooking basket and cook for 15 minutes, stirring them halfway. Flavour it with salt and pepper to taste before serving.

Nutrition: Calories 132; Fat 3g; Carbs 14g; Protein 12g

Maple Sage Pomegranate Squash

Preparation time: 10 minutes
Cooking time: 12 minutes
Servings: 1

Ingredients:
- 57g squash, peeled & sliced into 2 ½ cm pieces
- 1 tbsp olive oil
- .50 tbsp salt
- A handful of sage leaves
- .50 tbsp maple syrup
- 2 tbsp pomegranate seeds

Directions:
1. Mix the squash, .50 tbsp oil, and salt in a bowl.
2. Preheat the air fryer to 190°C. Place the squash in your air fryer basket and cook for 7 minutes.
3. Meanwhile, rub the sage with the remaining oil. Stir in the sage to the squash and cook for 5 minutes.

4. Transfer the squash to your bowl with maple syrup, and mix it well. Plate the squash and sprinkle pomegranate seeds before serving.

Nutrition: Calories 685; Fat 63g; Carbs 33g; Protein 3g

Tomato Avocado Wraps

Preparation time: 10 minutes
Cooking time: 5 minutes
Servings: 4

Ingredients:
- 8 vegan egg-roll wrappers
- 3 mashed avocados
- Half a tin of chopped tomatoes
- 5ml oil, + 10ml
- Salt & pepper to taste

Directions:
1. Preheat your air fryer to 180°C.
2. Mix the avocados, tomatoes, oil, salt, and pepper in a bowl.
3. Lay out the egg-roll wrappers and fill each one with the prepared mixture. Wrap it to secure the filling.
4. Spray the wraps with the remaining oil, arrange them in the cooking basket and cook for 5 minutes until crispy. Serve.

Nutrition: Calories 110; Fat 5g; Carbs 2g; Protein 5g

Spicy Cauliflower Stir-Fry

Preparation time: 15 minutes
Cooking time: 30 minutes
Servings: 4
Ingredients:
- 1 cauliflower, cut into florets
- 2 tbsp olive oil
- 1 and a half of onions, thinly sliced
- 5 cloves of garlic, sliced
- 1.5 tbsp tamari
- 1 tbsp rice vinegar
- .50 tbsp coconut sugar
- 1 tbsp sriracha
- Salt & pepper to taste
- 2 spring onion, chopped

Directions:
1. Preheat the air fryer to 177°C.
2. Mix the cauliflower and oil in a bowl. Add the cauliflower in your basket and cook within 10 minutes.
3. Stir in the onions to the cauliflower and cook for 10 minutes. Stir in garlic to the cauliflower and cook for 5 minutes.

4. Meanwhile, mix the tamari, sriracha, rice vinegar, coconut sugar, salt, plus pepper in your bowl. Stir the sauce mixture into the cauliflower and cook for 5 minutes.
5. Plate the cauliflower and garnish with the spring onion. Serve.

Nutrition: Calories 93; Fat 3g; Carbs 13g; Protein 3g

Courgette Burgers

Preparation time: 10 minutes
Cooking time: 12 minutes
Servings: 4

Ingredients:
- 1 courgette, grated & drain the excess water
- 1 small can of chickpeas, drained
- 3 spring onions, chopped
- A pinch of dried garlic
- Salt & pepper to taste
- 3 tbsp coriander
- 1 tsp chilli powder
- 1 tsp mixed spice
- 1 tsp cumin

Directions:
1. Mix the courgette, spring onions, chickpeas, zucchini and seasoning in a large bowl. Form this mixture into burgers.
2. Add the burgers in your basket and cook them for 12 minutes at 200ºC. Serve.

Nutrition: Calories 36; Fat 1g; Carbs 6g; Protein 3g

Mexican Bean Wraps

Preparation time: 10 minutes
Cooking time: 6 minutes
Servings: 2

Ingredients:
- 2 vegan Mexican tortillas
- 60g canned pinto beans, drained
- 60g grated vegan cheese
- 5/6 iceberg lettuce leaves
- 2 sliced avocados
- 60ml readymade salsa
- 5–10ml oil

Directions:
1. Preheat your air fryer to 180°C.
2. Arrange the beans, grated cheese, salsa, lettuce leaves and avocado slices on each tortilla.
3. Wrap the tortillas to secure the filling, and spray it with the oil.
4. Add the tortillas in your basket and cook within 6 minutes. Serve.

Nutrition: Calories 149; Fat 4g; Carbs 6g; Protein 6g

Crispy Vegan Ravioli

Preparation time: 15 minutes
Cooking time: 8 minutes
Servings: 4

Ingredients:
- 115g breadcrumbs
- 8g yeast flakes
- 4g dried basil
- 4g dried oregano
- 2 grated garlic cloves
- 60ml aquafaba liquid
- 225g vegan ravioli filled with any filling of your choice
- 150ml readymade Italian tomato sauce
- 10ml oil

Directions:
1. Preheat your air fryer to 190°C.
2. Mix the breadcrumbs, yeast flakes, dried basil, dried oregano, and garlic cloves in a bowl
3. Place the aquafaba in a separate bowl. Add the ravioli and lift out with a slotted spoon.
4. Coat the ravioli in the breadcrumb mixture, and spray it with oil.
5. Arrange the ravioli in the cooking basket and cook for 8 minutes, turning the ravioli halfway. Strain on a paper-towel-lined plate.
6. Stir the tomato sauce in your saucepan until heated. Serve the ravioli with a bowl of tomato sauce for dipping.

Nutrition: Calories 180; Fat 0g; Carbs 5g; Protein 2g

Lentil Burgers

Preparation time: 15 minutes
Cooking time: 1 hour & 20 minutes
Servings: 4

Ingredients:
- 100g black buluga lentils
- 1 carrot, grated
- 1 onion, diced
- 100g white cabbage, chopped
- 300g oats
- 1 tbsp garlic puree
- 1 tsp cumin
- Salt & pepper to taste
- Water, as needed

Directions:
1. Blend the oats in your blender until they resemble flour.
2. Add the lentils to a saucepan. Add some water and cook for 45 minutes.
3. Steam the vegetables for 5 minutes in a skillet with enough water until softened.

4. Mix all the fixings into your bowl and form this mixture into burgers.
5. Put the burgers in your basket and cook at 180ºC for 30 minutes. Serve.

Nutrition: Calories 509; Fat 8g; Carbs 40g; Protein 21g

Balsamic Summer Vegetables

Preparation time: 15 minutes
Cooking time: 8 minutes
Servings: 1

Ingredients:
- 30g zucchini, diced
- 30g yellow squash, diced
- 30g mushroom, diced
- 1 red onion, diced
- 30g sweet red pepper, diced
- 1 tbsp vegetable oil
- Salt & black pepper to taste
- 1 tbsp balsamic vinegar

Directions:
1. Preheat the air fryer to 180°C.
2. Mix the zucchini, yellow squash, mushroom, red onion, sweet red pepper, vegetable oil, vinegar, salt, and pepper in your large bowl.
3. Transfer the mixture to your basket, and cook the veggies within 8 minutes. Serve.

Nutrition: Calories 155; Fat 14g; Carbs 8g; Protein 2g

Pumpkin Fries

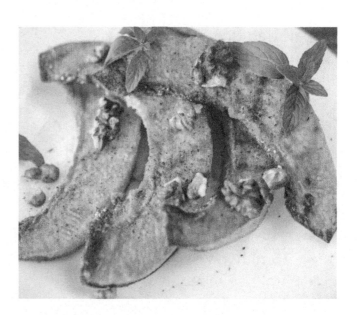

Preparation time: 5 minutes
Cooking time: 15 minutes
Servings: 4

Ingredients:
- 1 small pumpkin, seeds removed and peeled, cut into half-inch slices
- 2 tsp olive oil
- 1 tsp garlic powder
- .50 tsp paprika
- A pinch of salt

Directions:
1. Mix the pumpkin, olive oil, garlic powder, paprika, and salt in a large bowl.
2. Arrange the pumpkin slices in your cooking basket, and cook at 280ºC for 15 minutes until tender. Serve.

Nutrition: Calories 126; Fat 11g; Carbs 17g; Protein 14g

Tofu in Sesame Sauce

Preparation time: 20 minutes
Cooking time: 15 minutes
Servings: 4

Ingredients:
- 400g extra firm drained and dried tofu, diced
- 60ml orange juice
- 28g finely chopped spring onions
- 14 toasted sesame seeds
- 15ml honey
- 5ml rice vinegar
- 2g cornflour
- 50ml soy sauce
- 115g brown rice, cooked
- Salt & pepper to taste
- 5ml oil

Directions:

1. Preheat your air fryer to 180°C.
2. Spray the tofu with the oil until well coated. Add the tofu in your basket and cook within 15 minutes..
3. Stir the orange juice, spring onions, sesame seeds, honey, rice vinegar, cornflour, and soy sauce into a saucepan over medium heat until thickened.
4. Mix the tofu with the sauce and serve with brown rice.

Nutrition: Calories 160; Fat 2g; Carbs 12g; Protein 6g

Cauliflower Chickpea Tacos

Preparation time: 10 minutes
Cooking time: 20 minutes
Servings: 4

Ingredients:
- 256g cauliflower florets
- 404g can of chickpeas, drained and rinsed
- 2 tbsp olive oil
- 2 tbsp taco seasoning
- 8 corn tortilla
- 2 avocados sliced
- 280g cabbage, shredded
- Coconut yoghurt, as needed

Directions:
1. Preheat the air fryer to 198°C.
2. Toss the cauliflower, chickpeas, olive oil, and taco seasoning in a bowl.
3. Transfer the cauliflower mixture to the cooking basket and cook for 20 minutes.

4. Serve the cauliflower and chickpeas in tacos with avocado slices, cabbage, and coconut yoghurt.

Nutrition: Calories 507; Fat 15g; Carbs 76g; Protein 20g

Balsamic Brussels Sprouts

Preparation time: 10 minutes
Cooking time: 10 minutes
Servings: 2

Ingredients:
- 1 tbsp avocado oil
- .50 tsp salt
- .50 tsp pepper
- 400g Brussels sprouts halved
- 1 tsp balsamic vinegar

Directions:
1. Preheat the air fryer to 175ºC.
2. Mix the oil, salt, plus pepper in your bowl. Add the Brussels sprouts, and toss it well.
3. Add the sprouts in your basket and cook within 5 minutes. Shake the cooking basket, and cook again for 5 minutes. Sprinkle with balsamic vinegar before serving.

Nutrition: Calories 94; Fat 9g; Carbs 13g; Protein 5g

SNACKS AND APPETIZERS RECIPES

Avocado Fries

Preparation time: 15 minutes
Cooking time: 8 minutes
Servings: 4

Ingredients:
- 2 large, sliced avocados
- 110g flour
- 230g breadcrumbs
- 10ml water
- 5ml lemon juice
- 2 eggs
- 10ml oil
- Salt & pepper, as needed

Directions:
1. Preheat the air fryer to 200°C.
2. Mix the flour and breadcrumbs in a bowl.
3. Beat the egg in a second bowl, add the water and lemon juice, and mix it well.
4. Dip the avocado slices into the flour mixture, then in the egg mixture until well coated. Carefully lay the slices onto the flour mixture again until well coated.
5. Spray the avocado slices with oil, and add them in your basket, leaving gaps for the hot air to circulate. Cook within 8 minutes, and serve.

Nutrition: Calories 160; Fat 9g; Carbs 13g; Protein 5g

Sweet Potato Tots

Preparation time: 15 minutes
Cooking time: 8 minutes
Servings: 24 tots
Ingredients:
- 2 sweet potatoes, peeled
- .50 tsp Cajun seasoning
- Olive oil cooking spray
- Sea salt to taste

Directions:
1. Boil the sweet potatoes in your skillet within15 minutes. Let it cool.
2. Grate the sweet potato and mix it with Cajun seasoning. Form this mixture into tot-shaped cylinders.
3. Spray the cooking basket with oil, and arrange the tots inside.
4. Flavour them with salt and cook for 8 minutes at 200°C. Flip and cook again within 8 minutes. Serve.

Nutrition: Calories 21; Fat 0g; Carbs 4g; Protein 0g

Carrot Fries

Preparation time: 15 minutes
Cooking time: 20 minutes
Servings: 4

Ingredients:
- 4 carrots, peeled & sliced lengthwise
- 1 tbsp cornflour
- 1 tbsp paprika
- .50 tbsp garlic powder
- 1 tbsp olive oil
- Salt to taste

Directions:
1. Preheat the air fryer to 189°C.
2. Mix the carrots, cornflour, paprika, garlic powder, and olive oil in a bowl.
3. Transfer the seasoned carrots to the cooking basket and spread them in one layer without overlapping.

4. Cook the carrots for 20 minutes, flipping them halfway. Season it with salt before serving.

Nutrition: Calories 30; Fat 1g; Carbs 5g; Protein 1g

Courgette Meatballs

Preparation time: 15 minutes
Cooking time: 10 minutes
Servings: 4

Ingredients:
- 150g oats, pulsed in your blender until you have a breadcrumbs
- 40g feta, crumbled
- 1 egg, beaten
- Salt & pepper to taste
- 150g zucchini, grated & squeezed any excess water
- 1 tsp lemon rind
- 6 basil leaves, sliced thinly
- 1 tsp dill
- 1 tsp oregano

Directions:
1. Preheat the air fryer to 200°C.
2. Mix the zucchini, feta, egg, lemon rind, basil leaves, dill, oregano, salt, and pepper in a bowl.
3. Add the oats to the zucchini bowl and mix it well. Form them into balls, arrange them in the cooking basket, and cook for 10 minutes. Serve.

Nutrition: Calories 203; Fat 6g; Carbs 29g; Protein 9g

Asparagus Fries

Preparation time: 10 minutes
Cooking time: 6 minutes
Servings: 2

Ingredients:
- 1 egg
- 12 asparagus spears prepared
- 1 tsp honey
- 75g panko breadcrumbs
- Pinch of cayenne pepper
- 75g parmesan, grated
- 50g mustard
- 4 tbsp Greek yoghurt

Directions:
1. Preheat the air fryer to 200ºC.
2. Mix the egg and honey in a medium bowl. Pour the panko crumbs and Parmesan into a medium plate.
3. Coat each asparagus in the egg and then in the breadcrumbs. Add the asparagus in your basket and cook within 6 minutes.
4. Mix the cayenne pepper, mustard, and yoghurt in a bowl and serve with the asparagus fries.

Nutrition: Calories 188; Fat 2g; Carbs 9g; Protein 1g

Orange Sesame Cauliflower

Preparation time: 10 minutes + chilling time
Cooking time: 32 minutes
Servings: 4

Ingredients:
- 100ml water
- 30g cornflour
- 50g flour
- 1/2 tsp salt
- ½ tsp pepper
- 2 tbsp tomato ketchup
- 2 tbsp brown sugar
- 1 sliced onion

Directions:
1. Mix the flour, cornflour, water, salt, and pepper in a bowl. Coat the cauliflower with the flour mixture and keep it in your fridge for 30 minutes until firm.
2. Add the cauliflower your basket and cook at 170ºC for 22 minutes.
3. Meanwhile, mix the tomato ketchup, brown sugar, and onion in a saucepan, then gently simmer until thickened. Mix the cauliflower with the sauce, then serve.

Nutrition: Calories 236; Fat 21g; Carbs 14g; Protein 15g

Taco Hot Dogs

Preparation time: 10 minutes
Cooking time: 9 minutes
Servings: 2

Ingredients:
- 2 hot dogs
- 1 tbsp taco seasoning mix
- 2 hot dog buns
- 50g guacamole
- 4 tbsp salsa
- 6 slices of pickled jalapeno
- 1 lemon, halved

Directions:
1. Preheat the air fryer to 195°C.
2. Make 5 cuts on each hot dog, then rub them with the taco seasoning. Add the hot dogs in your basket and cook within 5 minutes.
3. Place the air-fried hot dogs in the buns and cook again for 4 minutes. Top the hot dog with guacamole, salsa, and jalapeno. Serve the taco hot dogs with lemon slices.

Nutrition: Calories 380; Fat 27g; Carbs 3g; Protein 34g

Cheese Stuffed Mushroom

Preparation time: 10 minutes
Cooking time: 8 minutes
Servings: 1

Ingredients:
- 31g fresh Portobello mushroom, cut off the stem and remove the mushroom flesh
- 28g cream cheese
- 1 tbsp parmesan cheese, shredded
- .50 tbsp sharp cheddar cheese, shredded
- .50 tbsp white cheddar cheese, shredded
- 1 tbsp Worcestershire sauce
- 1 garlic clove, minced
- Salt & black pepper to taste
- Parsley for garnishing

Directions:
1. Mix the cream cheese, Parmesan, all cheddar cheeses, Worcestershire sauce, garlic, salt, and pepper in your bowl. Preheat the air fryer to 185°C.
2. Fill the mushrooms with the prepared mixture, place them in the cooking basket, and cook for 8 minutes. Let it cool. Sprinkle the parsley on top and serve.

Nutrition: Calories 116; Fat 7g; Carbs 3g; Protein 8g

Potato Crisps

Preparation time: 10 minutes + soaking time
Cooking time: 15 minutes
Servings: 6

Ingredients:
- 2 large potatoes sliced into chips, soaked in water & patted dry
- 8g dried mixed herbs
- 2g sea salt
- 5ml oil

Directions:
1. Spray the potato chips with oil. Warm up your air fryer to 180°C.
2. Mix the salt and dried herbs in a small bowl, then sprinkle the mixture onto both sides of the potato slices.
3. Arrange the potato slices in the cooking basket and cook for 15 minutes each until crisp. Serve.

Nutrition: Calories 149; Fat 1g; Carbs 8g; Protein 1g

Shishito Peppers

Preparation time: 5 minutes
Cooking time: 10 minutes
Servings: 2

Ingredients:
- 200g shishito peppers
- Salt & pepper to taste
- .50 tbsp avocado oil
- 75g grated cheese

Directions:
1. Mix the shishito peppers, oil, salt, plus pepper in your bowl, then spray it with oil.
2. Add the shishito peppers in your basket and cook for 10 minutes at 175ºC. Transfer them to a plate and sprinkle them with cheese before serving.

Nutrition: Calories 286; Fat 4g; Carbs 1g; Protein 3g

Onion Rings

Preparation time: 10 minutes
Cooking time: 3 minutes

Servings: 4
Ingredients:
- 200g flour
- 75g cornflour
- 2 tsp baking powder
- 1 tsp salt
- 2 pinches of paprika
- 1 large onion, cut into rings
- 1 egg
- 1 cup milk
- 200g breadcrumbs
- 2 pinches garlic powder

Directions:
1. Stir the flour, salt, cornflour, and baking powder in a bowl. Dip each onion into the flour mixture until well coated.
2. Whisk the egg plus milk into the flour mixture, and dip in the onion rings. Lastly, dip the onion rings into the bread crumbs—Warm up the air fryer to 200ºC.
3. Arrange the onion rings in the cooking basket and cook within 2 to 3 minutes until golden brown. Sprinkle it with paprika and garlic powder to serve.

Nutrition: Calories 321; Fat 4g; Carbs 59g; Protein 10g

Celery Root Fries

Preparation time: 10 minutes
Cooking time: 10 minutes
Servings: 2
Ingredients:
- half of the celeriac, cut into pieces
- 600ml water
- 1 tbsp lime juice
- 1 tbsp olive oil
- 50g mayonnaise
- 1 tbsp mustard
- 1 tbsp horseradish, powdered

Directions:
1. Mix the celeriac, water and lime juice in your large bowl and soak the celeriac for 30 minutes.
2. Preheat the air fryer to 200ºC.
3. Mix the mayonnaise, horseradish and mustard in another bowl. Set aside in your fridge.
4. Drain the celeriac, drizzle with oil, and flavour it with salt plus pepper. Add the celeriac root fries in your basket and cook within 10 minutes. Serve.

Nutrition: Calories 168; Fat 12g; Carbs 13g; Protein 2g

Aubergine Parmesan

Preparation time: 10 minutes
Cooking time: 12-16 minutes
Servings: 4
Ingredients:
- 1 aubergine, sliced into rounds
- 100g Italian breadcrumbs

- 50g grated parmesan
- 1 tsp Italian seasoning
- 1 tsp salt
- .50 tsp dried basil
- .50 tsp onion powder
- .50 tsp black pepper
- 100g flour
- 2 eggs

Directions:
1. Mix the breadcrumbs, Parmesan, salt, Italian seasoning, basil, onion powder, and pepper in a bowl.
2. Put the flour to a second bowl, and beat the eggs in the last bowl. Coat the aubergine in the flour bowl, then in the eggs, and coat in the bread crumbs.
3. Preheat the air fryer to 185°C. Arrange the aubergine in the cooking basket and cook for 8 to 10 minutes. Turn it over and cook within 6 minutes.

Nutrition: Calories 286; Fat 26g; Carbs 25g; Protein 25g

Potato Kale Nuggets

Preparation time: 15 minutes
Cooking time: 14 minutes
Servings: 2
Ingredients:
- 150g potatoes, chopped, boiled & drained
- 130g kale, chopped
- .50 tbsp olive oil
- Half of the minced garlic clove
- 15ml almond milk
- .25 tbsp salt
- black pepper, as needed
- Vegetable oil spray

Directions:
1. Heat your skillet over medium heat, add the oil and sauté the garlic for 3 minutes.
2. Add the potatoes, garlic, almond milk, salt, and pepper to a bowl, then mash using a potato masher. Stir in the kale, and make 2 ½ cm nuggets with the potato-kale mixture.
3. Warm up your air fryer to 198°C and grease your cooking basket. Arrange the nuggets inside, and cook within 14 minutes. Serve.

Nutrition: Calories 380; Fat 27g; Carbs 3g; Protein 34g

Courgette Fries

Preparation time: 10 minutes
Cooking time: 10 minutes
Servings: 4
Ingredients:
- 1 courgette, cut into thin strips or spirals
- 220g breadcrumbs
- 1 egg

- 100g grated Parmesan cheese
- 4g Italian seasoning
- 5–10ml oil

Directions:

1. Preheat your air fryer to 200°C. Mix the cheese, breadcrumbs, and seasoning in your bowl. Beat the egg in a small bowl.
2. Dip the courgette strips into the egg mixture, then the breadcrumb mixture until well coated. Spray the strips with the oil.
3. Arrange the strips in the cooking basket, and cook for 10 minutes. Serve.

Nutrition: Calories 30; Fat 2g; Carbs 5g; Protein 2g

DESSERTS RECIPES

Chocolate Chip Biscuits

Preparation time: 10 minutes
Cooking time: 8-10 minutes
Servings: 12 biscuits

Ingredients:
- 115g melted butter
- 40g granulated sugar
- 10ml vanilla essence
- 1 beaten egg
- 190g plain flour
- 2g salt
- 2g baking powder
- 120g chocolate chips

Directions:
1. Warm up your air fryer to 170°C. Put a parchment paper in your cooking basket.
2. Beat the butter plus sugar in your bowl. Mix in the egg, vanilla essence, baking powder, flour, plus salt until smooth.
3. Mix in the chocolate chips. Arrange 12 scoops of evenly spaced biscuit dough on the air fryer, leaving 5 cm between each one.
4. Cook for 8 to 10 minutes until golden brown. Serve.

Nutrition: Calories 320; Fat 13g; Carbs 18g; Protein 4g

Key Lime Cheesecake

Preparation time: 15 minutes + chilling time
Cooking time: 30 minutes
Servings: 12
Ingredients:
- 750g soft cream cheese
- 75g melted butter
- 400g caster sugar
- 3 eggs
- 50ml Greek yoghurt
- 15ml vanilla essence
- 90g crushed biscuits
- Zest and juice of 8 limes

Directions:
1. Preheat your air fryer to 160°C. Spray the baking tin (fitted in your air fryer basket) with the oil and line it with parchment.
2. Mix the crushed biscuits with the butter using your hands. Place the biscuit mixture in the pan and press down firmly.
3. Whisk the sugar and cream cheese in a bowl until smooth. Add the yoghurt, vanilla essence

and lime ingredients, and beat again. Beat the eggs and mix in the cream cheese mixture.

4. Pour the batter on top of the biscuit base, arrange it in your air fryer basket, and cook for 30 minutes. Let it cool for 30 minutes.

5. Keep the cheesecake in the fridge overnight before removing it from the baking tin. Decorate with more lime zest before serving.

Nutrition: Calories 380; Fat 15g; Carbs 22g; Protein 3g

Chocolate Brownies

Preparation time: 10 minutes
Cooking time: 15 minutes
Servings: 4
Ingredients:
- 110g plain flour
- 84g unsweetened cocoa powder
- 170g sugar
- 60g unsalted butter
- 2 eggs
- 15ml oil
- 6ml vanilla essence
- 2g baking powder
- 5ml oil

Directions:
1. Preheat your air fryer to 160°C.
2. Spray the baking tin (fitted in your air fryer basket) with the 5ml oil and line it with parchment
3. Beat the eggs with flour, cocoa powder, sugar, butter, 15ml oil, vanilla essence, and baking powder in a bowl until smooth.

4. Pour the batter into the baking tin, arrange it in your air fryer basket, and cook for 15 minutes. Serve.

Nutrition: Calories 350; Fat 17g; Carbs 33g; Protein 9g

Wonton-Wrapped Banana Bites

Preparation time: 10 minutes
Cooking time: 6 minutes
Servings: 12
Ingredients:
- 1 banana, peeled & sliced
- 12 wonton wrappers
- 75g peanut butter
- 1-2 tsp vegetable oil
- 2 tbsp lemon juice

Directions:
1. Place the banana in a water bowl with lemon juice to prevent browning.
2. Arrange one piece of banana and a spoonful of peanut butter in each wonton wrapper. Wet the

edges of each wrapper and fold it over to seal.

3. Spray the air fryer basket with oil, arrange the wrapped bananas, and cook at 190ºC for 6 minutes. Serve.

Nutrition: Calories 386; Fat 26g; Carbs 20g; Protein 21g

Pistachio Brownies

Preparation time: 15 minutes
Cooking time: 20 minutes
Servings: 4
Ingredients:
- 75ml milk
- .50 tsp vanilla extract
- 25g salt
- 25g pecans
- 75g flour
- 75g sugar
- 25g cocoa powder
- 1 tbsp ground flax seeds

Directions:
1. Mix the salt, pecans, flour, sugar, cocoa powder, and flax seeds in a bowl. Whisk the milk and vanilla extract in a small bowl. Mix both mixtures until smooth.
2. Preheat the air fryer to 175ºC. Line a 5-inch cake tin with parchment paper. Pour the brownie mix into the cake tin, place it in your cooking basket and cook for 20 minutes. Serve.

Nutrition: Calories 486; Fat 26g; Carbs 25g; Protein 25g

Fruit Crumble

Preparation time: 10 minutes
Cooking time: 15 minutes
Servings: 2

Ingredients:
- 1 diced apple
- 75g frozen blackberries
- 25g brown rice flour
- 2 tbsp sugar
- .50 tsp cinnamon
- 2 tbsp butter

Directions:
1. Preheat the air fryer to 150ºC.
2. Mix the apple and blackberries in an air fryer-safe baking pan.
3. Mix the flour, sugar, cinnamon, and butter in a bowl, then spoon over the fruit. Put the pan in your basket, and cook within 15 minutes. Serve.

Nutrition: Calories 310; Fat 12g; Carbs 50g; Protein 2g

Shortbread Cookies

Preparation time: 15 minutes
Cooking time: 20 minutes
Servings: 12
Ingredients:
- 250g flour
- 75g sugar
- 175g butter
- 1 tbsp vanilla essence
- Chocolate buttons for decorating

Directions:
1. Preheat the air fryer to 180ºC
2. Mix the flour, sugar, butter, and vanilla essence in a bowl. Form a dough and roll it out to around 1cm thick. Cut the dough with your favourite cookie cutter.
3. Add the cookies in your basket and cook within 10 minutes. Place the chocolate buttons onto the shortbread and cook for another 10 minutes at 160ºC.

Nutrition: Calories 385; Fat 32g; Carbs 24g; Protein 18g

Nutty Granola Bars

Preparation time: 10 minutes
Cooking time: 20 minutes
Servings: 8
Ingredients:
- 70g chopped almonds
- 35g chopped pecans
- 100g shredded coconut
- 25g dried fruit
- 25g chocolate chips
- 40g sunflower seeds
- 15g melted butter
- 15ml maple syrup
- 15g granulated sugar
- 4ml vanilla essence
- 1g salt

Directions:
1. Preheat your air fryer to 150°C. Spray the air fryer tray with the oil and line it with parchment
2. Process the coconut, nuts and sunflower seeds until crumbled in your food processor. Mix it with the fruit, chocolate chips and salt in a bowl
3. Mix the butter and maple syrup in your small saucepan over low heat, then stir in the sugar and vanilla essence.
4. Pour the butter mixture over the granola crumbs, then mix thoroughly using your hands. Pour the mixture onto the air fryer tray and press down until the mixture is firm.
5. Cook it in your air fryer for 20 minutes. Serve.

Nutrition: Calories 260; Fat 8g; Carbs 0g; Protein 15g

Chocolate Sponge Cake

Preparation time: 15 minutes
Cooking time: 30 minutes
Servings: 6

Ingredients:
- 175g plain flour
- 45g cocoa powder
- 5g baking powder
- 80g granulated sugar
- 60g butter
- 60ml milk
- 2 eggs
- 5ml vanilla essence
- 2g salt
- 5ml oil

Directions:
1. Preheat your air fryer to 160°C. Spray the air fryer baking tin with the oil and line it with parchment.
2. Beat the butter plus sugar in your bowl. Whisk the eggs and pour it to the butter sugar mixture, then pour the milk and vanilla. Mix it until smooth.
3. Mix the flour, cocoa powder, baking powder, and salt in your separate bowl. Fold it into the batter in stages until the cake mixture is smooth.
4. Pour the batter into your baking tin and cook in your air fryer for 30 minutes. Serve.

Nutrition: Calories 300; Fat 15g; Carbs 12g; Protein 4g

Graham S'mores

Preparation time: 10 minutes
Cooking time: 5 minutes
Servings: 2

Ingredients:
- 2 graham crackers, broken in half
- 2 marshmallows, halved
- 2 pieces of chocolate

Directions:
1. Place 2 halves of graham crackers in the air fryer basket and add a marshmallow to each sticky side down.
2. Cook them at 180°C for 5 minutes until the marshmallows are golden. Remove, add a piece of chocolate and top it with another graham. Serve!

Nutrition: Calories 294; Fat 13g; Carbs 29g; Protein 3g

Nutella & Banana Sandwich

Preparation time: 10 minutes
Cooking time: 7 minutes
Servings: 2
Ingredients:
- A little softened butter for spreading
- 100g chocolate spread
- 4 slices of regular white bread
- 1 ripe banana, sliced

Directions:
1. Warm up your air fryer to 175ºC.
2. Butter one side of your bread, and spread the chocolate on the other side.
3. Add the banana on top of the chocolate spread. Place another slice of bread on top with the chocolate side down. Cut the sandwiches into 2 triangles.
4. Place them in the cooking basket and cook for 5 minutes. Flip it over and cook within 2 minutes. Serve.

Nutrition: Calories 376; Fat 32g; Carbs 19g; Protein 14g

Peachy Pies

Preparation time: 15 minutes
Cooking time: 12 minutes
Servings: 4

Ingredients:
- 1 pack of ready-to-roll pastry
- 2 peaches, peeled & chopped
- 3 tbsp sugar
- 1 tbsp lemon juice
- 1 tsp vanilla extract
- 1 tsp cornflour
- .25 tsp salt

Directions:
1. Mix the peaches, lemon juice, sugar and vanilla in a large bowl. Leave it to stand for 15 minutes.
2. Drain the peaches, keeping 1 tbsp of the liquid on one side. Mix the cornflour into the peaches until well combined.
3. Cut the pastry into 8 circles, and add the peach mixture. Brush the edges with water and fold over to form half-moons.
4. Crimp the edges to seal, and coat with cooking spray. Put it in your basket and cook at 170ºC for 12 minutes, until golden brown. Serve.

Nutrition: Calories 486; Fat 26g; Carbs 25g; Protein 25g

Apple Chips with Yogurt Dip

Preparation time: 15 minutes
Cooking time: 12 minutes
Servings: 4

Ingredients:
- 1 apple, sliced into chips
- 3 tbsp Greek yoghurt
- 1 tbsp almond butter
- 2 tsp oil
- 1 tsp cinnamon
- 1 tsp honey

Directions:
1. Coat the apple slices with cinnamon and oil in a bowl. Coat

the cooking basket with cooking spray and add the apple slices— Cook the apple slices for 12 minutes at 180ºC.
2. Mix the butter, honey and yoghurt in a small bowl, then serve with the apple chips.

Nutrition: Calories 104; Fat 3g; Carbs 17g; Protein 1g

Apple Fritters

Preparation time: 10 minutes
Cooking time: 0 minutes
Servings: 4

Ingredients:
- 225g self-raising flour
- 200g Greek yoghurt
- 2 tsp sugar
- 1 tbsp cinnamon
- 1 apple, peeled and chopped
- Cooking spray oil

Directions:
1. Mix the flour, yoghurt, sugar, cinnamon, and apple. Knead for about 3 to 4 minutes.
2. Line the cooking basket with parchment paper and spray it with oil.
3. Divide the fritter mix into four, flatten each portion, and add them in your basket. Cook at 185ºC for about 15 minutes, turning halfway. Serve.

Nutrition: Calories 305; Fat 1g; Carbs 66g; Protein 9g

Chocolate Mug Cake

Preparation time: 10 minutes
Cooking time: 0 minutes
Servings: 1

Ingredients:
- 30g self-raising flour
- 5 tbsp sugar
- 1 tbsp cocoa powder
- 3 tbsp milk
- 3 tsp coconut oil

Directions:
1. Mix the flour, sugar, cocoa powder, milk, and oil in a mug.
2. Heat the air fryer to 200ºC. Place the mug in the cooking basket and cook for 10 minutes. Serve.

Nutrition: Calories 501; Fat 9g; Carbs 87g; Protein 6g

Conclusion

Air Fryers have become an essential kitchen appliance, replacing the traditional deep fryer and giving users healthier options. They are a must-try for anyone looking to improve their cooking, whether they are just starting out or are more advanced in the kitchen. Air fryers allow you to cook almost any food while keeping it healthy, as they cook with little to no additional oil. Not only is the food healthier, but it also tastes better and is less messy to clean up. Overall, air fryers provide a great way to cook delicious food without all of the negatives that come with deep frying.

We hope this cookbook has been useful in providing you with tips and tricks on how to use your air fryer and introducing you to many different and delicious recipes. With air fryers becoming increasingly popular, there is no better time to invest in one and start cooking up delectable dishes! Not only are they healthier than deep-fried food, but they are easy to use, require minimal clean-up and can help you cook multiple dishes in one go.

A little bit of practice, some creative recipes, and a regular maintenance schedule will ensure that your air fryer remains in optimal condition, providing you with delicious meals for many years to come. So, go ahead and get cooking with confidence with your air fryer!

Printed in Great Britain
by Amazon

16749051R00045